Berlin
Travel Guide

Quick Trips Series

No part of this publication may be reproduced, stored in a retrieval system, or transmitted, in any form or by any means without the prior written permission of the publisher, nor be otherwise circulated in any form of binding or cover other than that in which it is published and without similar condition being imposed on the subsequent purchaser. If there are any errors or omissions in copyright acknowledgements the publisher will be pleased to insert the appropriate acknowledgement in any subsequent printing of this publication. Although we have taken all reasonable care in researching this book we make no warranty about the accuracy or completeness of its content and disclaim all liability arising from its use.

Copyright © 2016, Astute Press
All Rights Reserved.

Table of Contents

BERLIN — 6
- CUSTOMS & CULTURE 7
- GEOGRAPHY 9
- WEATHER & BEST TIME TO VISIT 10

SIGHTS & ACTIVITIES: WHAT TO SEE & DO — 13
- REICHSTAG 13
- KULTURFORUM 15
- OLYMPIC STADIUM (OYMPIASTADION) 17
- POTSDAMER PLAZA 19
- STAATSOPER (OPERA HOUSE), UNDER DEN LINDEN 21
- TIERGARTEN 22
- BERLIN ZOO 24
- BERLIN WALL MEMORIAL 26
- OBSERVATION DECK AT BERLINER FERNSEHTURM (TV TOWER) 27
- BERLINER DOM CATHEDRAL 29
- CHARLOTTENBURG PALACE & GARDENS 31
- BRANDENBURG GATE 32
- MUSEUM ISLAND 33
- BERLIN PHILHARMONIC 35
- BERLIN'S JEWISH HISTORY 36

BUDGET TIPS — 38

ACCOMMODATION 38
- Propeller Island City Lodge 39
- Ostel 40
- Ackselhaus 40
- Otto 41
- Michelberger Hotel 42

RESTAURANTS, CAFÉS & BARS 43
- Rogacki 43
- Konnopke's Imbiss 44
- Schneeweiss 45
- Fleischerei 46
- Renger-Patzsch 47

SHOPPING 47
- Potsdamer Platz Arcades 48
- KaDeWe 49
- Kurfürstendamm 49
- Alexanderplatz 50
- Harry Lehmann 51

KNOW BEFORE YOU GO — 53

ENTRY REQUIREMENTS 53
HEALTH INSURANCE 53
TRAVELLING WITH PETS 54
AIRPORTS 55
AIRLINES 57
CURRENCY 58
BANKING & ATMS 58
CREDIT CARDS 59
RECLAIMING VAT 59
TIPPING POLICY 60

- Mobile Phones 61
- Dialling Code 61
- Emergency Numbers 62
- Public Holidays 62
- Time Zone 63
- Daylight Savings Time 63
- School Holidays 63
- Trading Hours 64
- Driving Laws 64
- Smoking Laws 65
- Drinking Laws 66
- Electricity 66
- Tourist Information (TI) 67
- Food & Drink 67
- Websites 69

BERLIN TRAVEL GUIDE

Berlin

Berlin is a cosmopolitan metropolis with some of the most dynamic art, theatre, opera, and music in Europe. This is a modern city yet profoundly historic. Berlin is the capital of Germany and has fully overcome it cold war and wartime past.

BERLIN TRAVEL GUIDE

Berlin has all the attractions of a large city but without the hassle. It is a city with a difficult history, but a unique identity. Formerly two halves with opposing ideologies, Berlin has been reunited - and there's seemingly no trace of the former separation. The two cities are one, and have come together to create a vibrant society that is both unique and thriving.

It has been more than 20 years since the wall came down, and Berlin is now at the height of its Renaissance - rivaling great cities like New York, Paris, and London in regards to its development, and sometimes even surpassing them. For instance, Berlin possesses one of the best systems of public transportation in the world.

There's no limit to what this great European city has to offer. From dazzling and distinctive architecture, to a

BERLIN TRAVEL GUIDE

variety of brilliant museums, to history, to sports, to the arts - Berlin, Germany has everything you could want in a modern city. It's trendy, it's open-minded, it's breathtakingly beautiful.

🌍 Customs & Culture

Berlin is widely recognized as being the "creative city," because it boasts some of the most original art, architecture, theatre, and opera in the world. For the last 20 years, artists, musicians, and cultured aficionados have come to Berlin to take advantage of the up and coming opportunities that the city has to offer. Berlin is a city that has been reborn out of the ruins of war, and has rejuvenated itself entirely.

In addition to its worldly outlook, Berlin is very much a German city. It holds German values, traditions, and

BERLIN TRAVEL GUIDE

features memorable German food. Yet, somehow, Berlin is distinctive from other German cities. It manages to possess the German features that make a city great, but has a contemporary, European mindset that draws people in from all over the world.

Berlin is a city that has been given a "second chance" and Berliners are some of the most optimistic people on the planet, and as a result, are incredibly warm and inviting. It is no wonder that Berlin has drawn such an astounding influx of immigration over the past 20 years, people move to the city and it becomes their home, and they are able to assimilate into the community.

Berlin is truly a magnificent place. It is at the forefront of the art scene and a contemporary metropolis, yet contains a rich history that puts it on par with Paris, London, and

BERLIN TRAVEL GUIDE

Vienna. Visitors from all over the world can visit, cool their heels in a biergarten and strike up a conversation with a local, or spend days touring the hundreds of wonderful museums. It is a thriving culture, one certainly worth experiencing.

🌐 Geography

The capital city of Berlin, and the largest city in Germany, is located in Northeastern Germany approximately one hour from the border of Poland (60km) to the east and 2 hours from the Baltic Sea to the North. It is one of Germany's 16 states and boasts a population of approximately 3.5 million people, making it the seventh most populous urban region in the European Union.

The region surrounding Berlin is predominately woods and marshland as it is part of the Northern European

BERLIN TRAVEL GUIDE

Plain, an essential region for European topography. It is extremely fertile land, similar to the American midwest, and production on the plain is the highest across Europe for agriculture. Berlin is also connected to the lush Spree Valley along the river by the same name, which connects to the Havel River, a tributary to the lengthy Elbe. These waterways combine to make Berlin a thriving region, with decadent greenery and surprisingly clean air for a large city.

Berlin is a beautiful city that sprawls out in many directions. Finding a quality map is recommended; but, although it's on the larger side it's a very walkable city, and many of the best sites are best seen on foot. The public transportation is excellent and the neighborhoods are safe in comparison to other world cities.

BERLIN TRAVEL GUIDE

🌐 Weather & Best Time to Visit

Berlin is essentially a continental climate, slightly humid, with relatively hot summers and normally cold winters. It is not prone to bouts of extreme weather, and rests along a more moderate bent. In winter, temperatures range between -5 and 20 degrees Celsius, in spring from 0-32 Celsius, in summer from 12-37 Celsius, and in autumn from 2-34 Celsius. So, as long as you bring a jacket, there is never a bad time of year to be in Berlin.

The most idyllic time to take a trip to Berlin is from mid-May to the end of June. The temperatures are moderate, precipitation is low, and tourists have not begun their vacation. It is also the season of Berlin's grand festivals with Karneval der Kulturen, Christopher Street Day Parade, and many more.

BERLIN TRAVEL GUIDE

Whether you stay in Berlin for a weekend, a week, or a month, you will never run out of things to do. In early summer, visitors can take advantage of ideal weather on strolls through Berlin's many parks, eating in outdoor cafés and biergartens, and swimming in the crystal clear lakes under the sparkling German sun.

If you don't mind experiencing moderate cold, in Berlin cold winters are truly mild, the world famous Berlin International Film Festival occurs in February. This festival is on par with that of Cannes, and brings out an even livelier side of Berlin culture. It is Berlin's premiere festival, and although the days are slightly chilly, it's definitely an experience worth having.

BERLIN TRAVEL GUIDE

Sights & Activities: What to See & Do

🌏 Reichstag

Platz der Republik 1, 11011

Berlin, Germany

+030 22773107

http://www.bundestag.de/htdocs_e/index.html

The most stunning representation of the 1990

BERLIN TRAVEL GUIDE

Reunification of Germany at Berlin is in the renovated House of German Parliament (Bundestag) known as the Reichstag.

The original building was constructed between 1884 and 1894 after the unification of Germany under Otto Von Bismarck, as the country was in need of a proper house for the new government. Unfortunately, the first structure was badly damaged in a fire in the 1930s.

A temporary edifice was set up for the following 50 years, but with the reunification of Germany after the fall of the Berlin Wall, construction for a state of the art new Reichstag was set in motion, as a symbol of Germany's new political identity. The Bundestag hired renowned architect, Sir Norman Foster, to recreate the Reichstag, and the new building has been the seat of the German Parliament since 1999.

BERLIN TRAVEL GUIDE

The Reichstag is presently the second most visited building in Berlin and is one of the most easily recognized buildings in all of Germany. The most interesting point on the structure is the glass dome atop the apex of the building. From within, guests can walk along the stairwell and view Berlin in panorama; it is also possible to see the German Parliamentary seats from the interior of the dome.

Although it is an active government building, parts of the Reichstag are open year round to the public. An elevator near the entrance will take you to the rooftop where you can enter the dome and follow the spiral stairwell around the dome. The Reichstag is a brilliant tribute to the cultural triumph of Berlin, and a must see for every visitor to the capital.

BERLIN TRAVEL GUIDE

🌐 Kulturforum

Matthäikirchplatz 10785

Berlin, Germany

+030 266424242

http://www.kulturforum-berlin.de/

Berlin's Kulturforum is a collection of museums, buildings, and art collections that comprise Berlin's dynamic cultural epicenter. With a more contemporary focus, the Kulturforum is the modern correlation to Berlin's Museum Island. Located in the center of Berlin adjacent to Potsdamer Platz, the Kulturforum showcases the rising vitality of Berlin with a wide away of venues and museums. The buildings found within the region are the Neue Nationalgalerie, Museum of Decorative Arts, the Berlin State Library, and the Musical Instrument Museum, among others.

BERLIN TRAVEL GUIDE

The Neue Nationagalerie at the Kulturforum is Berlin's main museum for the exhibition of modern art. The galleries include pieces from the periods of Cubism, Surrealism, and Expressionism with a focus on the early 20th century. It's open to the public from 10:00 am to 6:00 pm and admission to the museum costs €10 for adults and €5 for children.

Another significant sight at the Kultruforum is the Gemäldegalerie Museum, which houses one of the most magnificent collections of Medieval and Renaissance art in all of Europe. Within its galleries visitors can view pieces from Van Eyck, Raphael, Rembrandt, and many others. Admission to the museum is €8 and it is open to the public from 10:00 am to 6:00 pm.

BERLIN TRAVEL GUIDE

Ultimately, the Kulturforum is a magnificent place to witness first hand the contemporary contributions of European art, encased in a style that is unique to Berlin.

🌑 Olympic Stadium (Oympiastadion)

Olympischer Platz 14053

Berlin, Germany

+030 30688100

http://www.olympiastadion-berlin.de/

The impressive Olympic Stadium in Berlin was built in the 1930's for the purpose of serving the 1936 Summer Olympics in Germany. It has been used by political figures, Olympiads, and more recently as a stadium for football - specifically for the FIFA World Cup in 1974 and 2006. There is much more to the stadium than just the

BERLIN TRAVEL GUIDE

arena, however, and the ground include the grand lawns known as Maifeld, the Waldbühne Forest Theater, and the Langemarck Halle.

The May Field (German, Maifeld) was built under as a green space for Olympic outdoor competitions and a number of May Day celebrations. It's capacity is for 250,000, and in 2012 the field became the official home of the Berlin Cricket Cup. Also housed on May Field grounds is a historic bell that used to be housed in a tall bell tower in the stadiums of May Field, but the structure was destroyed during the Second World War. The Langemark-Halle corridor is a commemoration of the 1914 Battle of Langemark in Germany, and also exhibits information concerning the original Reichssportfield (Olympiapark) of the 1930s.

BERLIN TRAVEL GUIDE

On the riverbanks of the Berlin glacial valley lies the Waldbühn Forest Theater which was built alongside the Olympic Stadium as a venue for concerts and cultural performances. It is still used today for similar purposes.

The Olympic Stadium is open to the public year round and provides guided tours for guests who wish to see the stadium and learn about its unique history. Prices for admission are €7.

🌐 Potsdamer Plaza

Linkstraße 2

10785 Berlin, Germany

+49 30 688315-0

http://potsdamerplatz.de/en/

Arguably the liveliest section of the city of Berlin,

BERLIN TRAVEL GUIDE

Potsdamer Plaza is an exciting square that's home to a variety of art, entertainment venues, and remarkable architecture. More than 100,000 visitors come to Potsdamer Plaza each day to enjoy activities in the square, and to take part in the culture of Berlin. It is situated close to the Brandenburg Gate and the Reichstag, and is part of the center of life in the city of Berlin.

Potsdamer Plaza hosts a selection of unique restaurants, boutique hotels, some of the city's best shopping, and a large amount of annual events and festivals. Also in the plaza is the Cinemaxx which contains 19 theaters and is ultimately the largest presentation of film in Berlin on a daily basis. Also in the plaza is Speilbank Berlin, a casino, with roulette and blackjack tables among many other forms of entertainment (admission to the Casino is €2.50).

BERLIN TRAVEL GUIDE

A premiere art exhibit in Potsdamer Plaza can be found at Panorama Point, which not only offers jaw-dropping views of the cityscape, but also hosts galleries telling the story, in photos, of the particular history of Berlin's Potsdamer Plaza. But Panorama Point is not the only art showcase in the Plaza, there are multiple galleries in the area.

No matter what your fancy is - whether it's shopping, art, entertainment, or food - you can find it Berlin's contemporary cultural epicenter in Potsdamer Plaza.

🌐 Staatsoper (Opera House), Under Den Linden

Bismarckstraße 110 10625

Berlin, Germany

030 2035-4555

BERLIN TRAVEL GUIDE

http://www.staatsoper-berlin.org/en_EN/

Nothing represents the rising cultural status of Germany's capital city like a night at the Berlin Opera, and few buildings showcase both the musical and architectural standards of the international city like the Staatsoper Under Den Linden (Berlin State Opera). Housed in a magnificent building in the Mitte District of east Berlin, the State Opera offers professional performances of Opera, comparable to those seen in prestigious opera houses all over the world.

Felix Mendelssohn, Richard Strauss, among many other renowned musicians have worked and performed in this grand opera house, and the venue continues to showcase the best of German music and opera today. Since the reunification of Germany and the fall of the Berlin Wall,

BERLIN TRAVEL GUIDE

the theatre has brought some of the most famous musicians, conductors, and performers from all over the world to play at Schiller Theater in East Berlin.

Like typical theater seasons, shows are performed from September to May and current and up and coming programs include Puccini's Tosca and Verdi's La Traviata. Prices vary depending on shows, but many start at as low as €14. Prices go up the closer to the show date, so reserving tickets early is the best way to go. It's truly an experience that every lover of art and music should participate in, and what better place to do it than the rising international city of Berlin.

🌐 Tiergarten

Straße des 17. Juni 100

10557 Berlin

BERLIN TRAVEL GUIDE

http://www.berlin.de/orte/sehenswuerdigkeiten/tiergarten/index.en.php

The Berlin Tiergarten (Animal Garden) is more than just a lush park with quaint walkways, it refers to the entire district housing Germany's Bundestag, the Parliamentary government. However, the actual Tiergarten Park is a favorite spot among Berlin locals for a mid-afternoon walk, picnic, or cycling. It is Berlin's largest inner city park.

Originally it was used as royal hunting grounds but fell into disuse during the war and throughout the restoration period. But after a period of renovation, as a result of Berlin's reunification during the 1990s, the park was brought back to life. It has rapidly become one of Berlin's best spots for outdoor recreation. It is approximately 520

BERLIN TRAVEL GUIDE

acres, making it the second largest urban park in Germany - Munich's Englischer Garden being first.

The park is bordered along the northern side by the German river Spree and is adjacent to the Berlin zoo. It is also considerably close to the Brandenburg Gate, Reichstag, Soviet War Memorial, ad the Potsdamer Platz. Visitors are encouraged to wander through its greenery en route to seeing the sights of Berlin, or to rest in the shade near the tiny lake near the center. The Berlin Tiergarten is the perfect place to stop and relax, and to take a moment from the bustle of the busy metropolis.

🌍 Berlin Zoo

Hardenbergplatz 8 10787

Berlin, Germany

+030 254010

BERLIN TRAVEL GUIDE

http://www.zoo-berlin.de

Situated next to Berlin's Animal Garden (Tiergarten) in the heart of the city, the Berlin Zoo offers an afternoon excursion that's fun and educational for children of all ages. The park boasts a selection of animal life from all over the world, in addition to a remarkable aquarium on the same grounds. It is the oldest zoo in the country of Germany, and with more that 1500 different species presented is arguably the most complete collection in the world.

It is also the most famous zoo in Europe as it sees more than 3 million visitors annually. What is also remarkable about the Zoological Gardens is its exquisite focus on breeding, a work attached to the collective work of local and international universities, in addition to other zoos

BERLIN TRAVEL GUIDE

from around the world. Its contributions have significantly aided the development of endangered species on the continent, and also has helped to raise awareness of animal endangerment practices throughout Germany.

Currently housed at the zoo are populations of rare deer, pigs, rhinoceros, and polar bears among many other. The Aquarium on the sites boasts over 9,000 species of animal life and a collection of rarities as well, rivaling some of the best aquariums in the world.

The zoological gardens are open from 9:00 am to 5:00 pm daily, sometimes later depending on the season, and costs around €13 for just the zoo and €20 for a combined Zoo/Aquarium ticket. Discounted tickets are available for large groups, children, and students.

BERLIN TRAVEL GUIDE

🌐 Berlin Wall Memorial

Bernauer Straße 111/119

13355 Berlin

+49 (0)30 467 98 66 66

http://www.berliner-mauer-gedenkstaette.de/en/

There is nothing more innate, more decorated, more essential to the culture of the international city of Berlin then the former Berlin Wall.

Berlin used to be a war torn city, a divided city, with completely opposing ideologies on either side. Soviet Ruled Berlin to the East, Free Germany to the West. But the two sides were reunited at last, in a victorious even that forever changed the future of Germany's capital. The wall fell. Communism was over - and the whole of Berlin

BERLIN TRAVEL GUIDE

could be free to taste the riches of that freedom, and coexist together in harmony.

The Berlin Wall Memorial is an anthem to the progress of the city of Berlin, dedicated to the reunification, and a reminder of the collective strength of the German people. It marks the center of the city, the middle of Berlin, and the memorial and museum has seen a tremendous influx of visitors to the site since its establishment in 2006. There is an extensive museum on the site as well, with exhibits showcasing the history of the Berlin Wall and also commemorates those who fell there during Soviet Rule.

The museum and memorial is open year round to the public and offers free admission and guided tours. Open hours are 9:30 am to 6:00 pm in the winter season, and 9:30 am to 7:00 pm in the summer season.

BERLIN TRAVEL GUIDE

🌍 Observation Deck at Berliner Fernsehturm (TV Tower)

Panoramastraße 1A

10178 Berlin - Germany

+49 (0)30 / 242 59 22

http://www.tv-turm.de/en/

Fernsehturm stands tall as a symbol of the city of Berlin, and is officially the tallest structure in the country of Germany.

Standing over 200 meters, the Fersehturm TV Tower offers the most spectacular panorama of the Berlin cityscape; and from its apex visitors can see the entire region of the capital with all of its extraordinary attractions.

BERLIN TRAVEL GUIDE

Built in the Sixties by the German Democratic Republic, the TV Tower was created as an example of the Soviet Union's power; but after the fall of Communism the structure has come to represent something else entirely. The TV Tower forms the skyline of the magnificent city of Berlin, and stands now as an architectural achievement demonstrating the strength of Berlin as a free, united city.

More than a million people take the elevator to the top of the tower each year making the TV Tower one of the most popular attractions in the city of Berlin.

The tower is open to the public from March to October from 9:00 am to midnight, and from November to February from 10:00 am to midnight. Tickets cost €12 for everyone older than 3. There is also a restaurant at the top of the tower, offering a mealtime experience amidst the 360-degree view of the city of Berlin. But, if you want to go, make a reservation, as seating is limited.

🌐 Berliner Dom Cathedral

Am Lustgarten

10178 Berlin (Mitte), Germany

+49 (0) 30 / 20269-136

http://www.berlinerdom.de/index.php?lang=en

A visit to the largest church in the city of Berlin, is a transcendent step into an otherworldly place of antiquity. It is an active sanctuary, and a central hub to the Protestant Church of Germany. Berlin Cathedral is designed in beautiful gothic stylings. The original structure, first constructed in 1465, was badly damaged during the Second World War. The current building was

BERLIN TRAVEL GUIDE

reconstructed to its current grandeur beginning in 1875 and completed, with some difficulty in 1996.

Arguably, the most remarkable feature found in the current cathedral is the ornately reconstructed 7,000 pipe pipe organ. Upon entering the grand cathedral, the eyes of visitors are instantly drawn to this magnificent piece of art that inhabits the back wall of the interior of the sanctuary.

Berliner Cathedral as a a whole was modeled after the Catholic cathedral, St. Peter's Basilica in Rome, to stand as a tribute to German Protestantism. Currently, guests are welcome to attend church services, take part in ceremonies, or to tour the extravagant buildings on guided tours. These guided tours are given Monday through Saturday from 9:00 am to 8:00 pm, and on

BERLIN TRAVEL GUIDE

Sundays and holidays from 12:00 pm to 8:00 pm.

Admission prices are set at €7.

🌍 Charlottenburg Palace & Gardens

Spandauer Damm 10 14059

Berlin, Germany

+030 320911

http://www.spsg.de/index.php?id=134

The Charlottenburg Palace and surround Gardens are a magnificent example of German baroque architecture and design. Constructed at the end of the 17th century, during the Prussian empire, as the official residence for the royal Hohensollern family. It is presently the largest palace in Germany's capital, and one of the last remaining vestiges of imperial Prussia.

BERLIN TRAVEL GUIDE

Another significant aspect of the palace grounds are the luxurious gardens surrounding the structure. They were designed in 1697 in a baroque style, complementary to the palace itself, and stylized after the gardens at the Palace in Versailles. In addition to the magnificent beauty of the gardens, the palace interior is home to one of the largest collection of art in the whole of Berlin.

The Palace and Garden are open to the public Tuesday through Sunday from 10:00 am to 6:00 pm and costs €10 to enter.

🌐 Brandenburg Gate

Pariser Platz 10117

Berlin, Germany

+030 250025

BERLIN TRAVEL GUIDE

http://www.brandenburgertor.de/

This iconic structure is recognized the world over as being synonymous with the city of Berlin. It was constructed during the Prussian Empire as the official gate to the city and redesigned two centuries later as its current representation, a triumphal arch. As was most of Berlin during this time, it was badly damaged during the Second World War and underwent reconstruction in the early 2000s.

Modeled after the Acropolis in Athens, the Brandenburg Gate is a stunning example of neoclassical architecture in modern Berlin. Until the fall of Communism in 1990, the gate was officially part of the Berlin wall, separating Communist east from free west. Now, after the reunification, it is celebrated as a grand landmark of free

BERLIN TRAVEL GUIDE

Berlin, and continues to be one of the most visited monuments in Berlin today. By day or by night, the gate is visible from many parts of town, standing firm as a statement to German freedom.

There is no admission fee for the monument, and it is located in the Unter den Linden region of Berlin.

Museum Island

Museumsinsel (Bodestraße)

10178 Berlin, Germany

+030 20 90 55 77

www.smb.museum/

Berlin is one of Europe's premiere cities for art and culture, and nowhere in the city is this better represented than on the marvelous Museum Island. Located in the

BERLIN TRAVEL GUIDE

Spree River, Museum Island is home to five different museums with five unique focuses. The Altes Museum (Old Museum) features the collection of classical antiquities of the Berlin State Museums. Opposing the Altes Museum is the Neues Museum (New Museum) which hosts a variety of pieces from ancient Egypt and prehistory. The Neues Museum received a RIBA award in 2010 for its magnificent neoclassical architecture.

Also housed on Museum Island are the Alte Nationalgalerie, Bode Museum, and the Pergamon Museum. The latter of these three is significant as it hosts one of the largest collections of original sized monuments from Middle Eastern Antiquity.

The Museum Complex was added to UNESCO's list of World Heritage Sites in 1999 for good reason. Visitors can

BERLIN TRAVEL GUIDE

spend days on the island exploring the vast treasures contained within the exquisite neoclassical buildings. The museum complex is open daily, and tickets are sold for €10 - typically, one ticket will grant you access to all five museums on the island within a particularly time frame.

Berlin Philharmonic

Herbert-von-Karajan-Straße 1

Berlin, Germany

+030 25488999

www.berliner-philharmoniker.de/

Listed as number three on the ranking of ten best European Orchestras on the continent, the Berlin Philharmonic is one of the world leaders of music performers in the world today. With a legacy extending back almost 150 years, and a resumé including Hans

BERLIN TRAVEL GUIDE

Richter, Richard Strauss, and Johannes Brahms - a night listening to a concert performed by the Berlin Philharmonic is an experience unmatched by much of the known world.

The primary concert venue for the Berlin Philharmonic is the Philharmonie, which after a fire, was reconstructed to its current grandeur. The present conductor for the orchestra is Sir Simon Rattle. Season for the Berlin Philharmonic runs from September to May, and tickets range from €25 - €72. During the summer, the company can be found touring throughout the world.

🌐 Berlin's Jewish History

Lindenstraße 9-14 10969

Berlin, Germany

030 25993300

BERLIN TRAVEL GUIDE

http://www.jmberlin.de/

A tour of the history of Berlin would not be complete without including the dramatic, tumultuous two thousand years of history of the German Jews- and there's no better place to do just that but the Museum of Jewish History in Berlin. The galleries contained within are some of the largest and most comprehensive collections in the whole of Europe. There is a select number of fixed exhibits in addition to a few rotating ones, featuring elements of Jewish history from Berlin, the whole of Germany, and select parts of Jewish history throughout the world.

The museum is open to the public year round from 10:00 am to 10:00 pm Mondays, and from 10:00 am to 8:00 pm Tuesday through Sunday. The Price of admission is €5.

BERLIN TRAVEL GUIDE

Budget Tips

🌍 Accommodation

Berlin is a rising international city recognized for its daring art scene and incredible culture. With eclectic architecture and an open-minded worldview, even a stay in Berlin is sure to be a step into a different universe.

From wacky lodges, to hotels encased in verdant gardens, to standard accommodations with breathtaking

BERLIN TRAVEL GUIDE

views of the cityscape, Berlin offers its guest a wide array of locations to rest a while in luxury and style. No matter what your tastes or budget, Berlin has the perfect place for you to stay while on vacation.

Propeller Island City Lodge

Albrecht-Achilles-Straße 58

10709 Berlin, Germany

+030 8919016

http://www.propeller-island.com/

€75-€115

The eclectic stylings of Propeller Island City Lodge are some of the most unique in all of Berlin, and the rest of the world for that matter. The rooms are surreal, otherworldly, and a night's stay is truly an artistic experience. Located in Charlottenburg, in the west of

BERLIN TRAVEL GUIDE

Berlin, Propeller Island offers standard amenities in addition to rooms that have been designed to amaze the visitors. For example, hotel patrons can choose between a coffin in a crypt, green padded cell, and various other oddities of similar characteristics.

Ostel

Wriezener Karree 5

10243 Berlin

+49 30 25 76 86 60

http://www.ostel.eu/en/index.html

€9-€50

One of the least expensive, but most original, accommodations in all of Berlin is the 1970's style themed Ostel in the eastern region of the city. Commonly referred to as a German Democratic Republic "Platten" Building,

Ostel offers a curiously delightful selection of rooms designed to fit any personality.

Located in the Mitte District, Ostel is a hotel that's suitable for young people of all ages, looking for a unique place to stay on their visit to Berlin.

Ackselhaus

Belforter Straße 21

10405 Berlin, Germany

Telephone

http://www.ackselhaus.de/

€130-€150

Widely reviewed as being both ingenious and unconventional, Ackselhaus is an excellent place to stay during any visit to Berlin. The rooms are charming with

BERLIN TRAVEL GUIDE

original decorations, and the grounds sport a lush inner garden a series of magnificent aquariums. It's a picturesque setting offering seclusion from the busy city. And it's good to know that they serve one of the latest, longest, and best breakfasts amongst hotels in Berlin.

Otto

Knesebeckstraße 10,

Berlin, Germany

Telephone

http://www.hotelotto.com

€60-€90

Located in the peaceful, quieter area of Berlin known as Charlottenburg, Hotel Otto offers accommodations with spectacular views of the city, free tea and coffee, and comfortable accoutrements.

BERLIN TRAVEL GUIDE

The atmosphere is inviting, the breakfast buffet on the 7th floor leaves nothing to be desired, and the staff is friendly. The rooms are modest but clean, and the hotel is only a short walk from the fantastic public transit of Berlin. Great prices, quality amenities, a stay at Otto is everything you need during your stay in Berlin.

Michelberger Hotel

Warschauer Straße 39/40

Berlin, Germany

+030 2977-8590

http://www.michelbergerhotel.com/

€70-€110

Traveler's Choice 2012 Winner for Trendiest Hotel, Michelberger is an unconventional place to spend your

BERLIN TRAVEL GUIDE

nights while on vacation in Berlin. Offering unique rooms in original styles, an enthusiastic staff, and a great café, you're sure to be living in style while at the Michelberger.

🌍 Restaurants, Cafés & Bars

The food culture of Berlin is just as eccentric, and just as wonderful as the rest of the features of the capital city. With influences from Russia, Turkey, Germany, and other notable European culinary flavorings, Berlin cuisine offers a unique taste of its international ideals.

Boasting original versions Currywurst and Schnitzel and gyros, and a phenomenal beer selection both imported and local, the culinary ideals of Berlin leave nothing to be desired. Whether you choose street food or fine dining, your unique tastes will be accommodated in Germany's rich capital.

BERLIN TRAVEL GUIDE

Rogacki

Wilmersdorfer Straße 145/146

10585 Berlin-Charlottenburg, Germany

030 343825-0

http://www.rogacki.de/

€0-€10

This incredible deli in the Charlottenburg District of Western Germany offers sensational products and remarkable prices. Situated in a former stable, Rogacki serves up 150 types of cheese, an otherworldly assortment of fresh meats, baked breads, local beer and wine. It is an authentic spot for delicious German food and a popular place among locals for lunch. A meal at Rogacki is a taste of German's rich culinary history, a

BERLIN TRAVEL GUIDE

feast for your senses, and one of the absolute best in the city of Berlin.

Konnopke's Imbiss

Schönhauser Allee 44 B

10435 Berlin, Germany

+030 4427-765

www.konnopke-imbiss.de

€1.25-€3.50

One of the cheapest, most delicious eats in all of Berlin, Konnopke's Imbiss offers a unique take on the typical frankfurter. Specializing in a style of food known as currywurst, a meal at this unconventional spot - situated beneath the U-Bahn - is an experience like anything else in Europe. Visitors can enjoy German style currywurst,

BERLIN TRAVEL GUIDE

fresh french fries, and various other snacks while reading the paper under the tracks at Konnopke's Imbiss.

Schneeweiss

Simplonstrasse 16,

Berlin, 10245, Germany

http://www.schneeweiss-berlin.de/schneeweiss.html

€8-€16

Chic, trendy, and delicious, Schneeweiss is a restaurant with incredible ambiance in addition to tasty eats. It's a spot that serves up modern German fare that's slightly different from the typical offerings found in pubs in Berlin.

It's fine dining at reasonable prices. The staff is friendly, the atmosphere inviting, and because of its location slightly off the beaten path, you can easily get a good meal while simultaneously avoiding the typical tourist crowds.

Fleischerei

Schönhauser Allee 8, Prenzlauer Berg,

Berlin, 10119 Germany

+030/501-82117

http://www.fleischerei-berlin.com/

€8-€27

Located in an old-timey butcher shop, Fleischerei is an authentic German meat lovers paradise. It is an upscale bistro with unconventional decor and food that will wow you. Although not particularly vegetarian friendly, the cuisine at Fleischerei is fresh, local, and contains standards well above many of the meat houses in Berlin.

So, if you're craving a steak in the capital of Germany, Fleischerei is the place to be.

Renger-Patzsch

Wartburgstr. 54, Schoeneberg,

Berlin, 1082 Germany

+ 030/784-2059

http://www.renger-patzsch.com/

€10-€25

This eclectic dining establishment in the Charlottenburg District of Berlin is a biergarten offering sensational food at affordable prices. Decorated in black and white photographs taken by a German photographer that the restaurant is named for, Renger-Patzsch is a delightful eating experience that can satisfy a variety of individual tastes. With choices like quail, braised lamb, and local

BERLIN TRAVEL GUIDE

wines - your senses are sure to be delighted during a meal at Renger-Patzsch.

🌐 Shopping

As a distinctive European city with a diversity of influences, Berlin is one of the finest places in Germany for shopping. Its extraordinary style, contemporary fashion, and brilliant art provide a unique experience for the average and professional shopper. Boasting everything from renowned designer wear from across the continent, to local artisans creating indigenous wares - Berlin is a magnificent place to be if you're looking for that perfect something.

Potsdamer Platz Arcades

10785 Berlin-Tiergarten, Potsdameer Platz 1

Berlin, Germany

BERLIN TRAVEL GUIDE

With more than 130 stores in this splendid area, centered adjacent to the beautiful Tiergarten and the Potsdamer Platz square, the Potsdamer Platz Arcades offer an optimal selection for an afternoon of shopping in Berlin. Whether you're looking for electronics, jewelry, clothes, or just something different to bring back home with you, you're sure to find it at the Potsdamer Platz Arcades. And what's more, after you're finished shopping for the day, you can head to the Cinestar close by for a taste of German film.

KaDeWe

Tauentzien Straße 21-24,

10789 Berlin Germany

+030 21210

http://www.kadewe.de/

BERLIN TRAVEL GUIDE

For international lovers of fashion, the eclectic, trendy KaDeWe is the place for you. With offerings from high end designers and a cutting-edge appeal, KaDeWe is a respected institution for fashion not only in Germany but in all of Europe.

It has been at its location for more than 100 years, and is the largest department store on the European Continent. And what's more: there's a food court located on the upper level with a rooftop café, so patrons can sate the hunger worked up from all that incredible shopping.

Kurfürstendamm

Kurfürstendamm 69

10707 Berlin, Germany

+030 8836970

BERLIN TRAVEL GUIDE

www.kurfuerstendamm.de

The shopping district of Kurfürstendamm is recognized as the 5th Avenue of Berlin for its wide selection of shops offering everything from designer wear to jewelry and unique souvenirs. It is a great spot, tending to cater to a younger audience, while retaining its elitist flair. The former high-end district of Berlin, Kurfürstendamm is a premiere shopper's paradise with stores including Yves Saint Laurent, H&M, amongst many other acclaimed international labels.

Alexanderplatz

Mitte District, East Berlin

10178, Germany

One of the many public squares in Berlin, Alexanderplatz

BERLIN TRAVEL GUIDE

is an epicenter for activity - eating, dancing, entertainment, and shopping.

Located in the trendy Mitte District in eastern Berlin, and affectionately called "Alex" by locals, the region offers a diversity of stores, department and independent, designed to fit the needs of an immense population. Not only is it a hotspot for German history and architecture, but it contains one of the largest department stores in Berlin, "The Kaufhof Group." Also in the square is the famous TV Tower.

Harry Lehmann

Kantstrasse 106

Berlin, Germany

+030 324 3582

www.parfum-individual.de

BERLIN TRAVEL GUIDE

The aroma at Harry Lehman reaches you long before you entered through the door. Within this magnificent, charming shop visitors are met with the sights and the smells of years long past. Harry Lehmann is a perfumery, creating original, natural scents like they have been created for a century. It is a family run operation, and so unique that no shopping extravaganza in Berlin is complete without a stop in this store.

BERLIN TRAVEL GUIDE

Know Before You Go

🌐 Entry Requirements

By virtue of the Schengen agreement, travellers from other countries in the European Union do not need a visa when visiting Germany. Visitors from Australia, Canada and the USA, do not require a visa, provided their stay does not exceed 90 days and that their passports are valid for at least three months after their stay in Germany ends. Travellers requiring a Schengen visa will be able to enter Germany with it multiple times within a 6 month period, if their stay does not exceed 90 days. They will also need to prove that they have sufficient funds to cover the duration of their stay. For a stay exceeding 90 days, non-EU visitors will need to apply for a temporary residence permit.

🌐 Health Insurance

Citizens of other EU countries are covered for emergency health care in Germany. UK residents, as well as visitors from Switzerland are covered by the European Health Insurance Card (EHIC), which can be applied for free of charge. Germany has

BERLIN TRAVEL GUIDE

excellent health care facilities, but emergency medical care can be expensive and will not be covered by the public health insurance of most non-European countries so health insurance cover should be obtained before leaving home. Visitors from non-Schengen countries will need to show proof of private health insurance that is valid for the duration of their stay in Germany (that offers at least €37,500 coverage), as a requirement of their visa application process.

🌐 Travelling with Pets

Germany participates in the Pet Travel Scheme (PETS) which allows UK residents to travel with their pets without requiring quarantine upon re-entry. When travelling with pets from another European Union country, your pet will need to have the correct documentation in the form of a pet passport. Certain conditions will need to be met. The animal will have to be microchipped and up to date with rabies vaccinations. Your pet will need to have had a rabies vaccination at least 21 days before your departure for Germany. If travelling from a high risk country, you will also need to submit the results of a Blood Titer test taken one month after vaccination and at least 3 months before your travel date. The animal needs to be identified either with a microchip or have an identifying tattoo.

BERLIN TRAVEL GUIDE

🌐 Airports

There are two airports that serve the international gateway of Berlin. **Berlin Tegel Airport** (TXL) is the larger of the two and the 4th busiest airport in Germany. Originally a military base, it was used in the Berlin Airlift operation in 1949. Towards the end of the 1950s, it began to replace Tempelhof Airport. The other main airport servicing Berlin is **Berlin Schönefeld Airport**, (SXF), once the major airport servicing East Berlin. Frankfurt Airport (FRA) is the busiest **Frankfurt Airport** (FRA) is the busiest airport in Germany and the third busiest in Europe. Located about 12km southwest of Frankfurt, it connects visitors with the densely populated Frankfurt/Rhine-Main region. Frankfurt was home to the world's first airport and airline in 1908, but this was replaced by the current airport around 1936 when it grew too small to handle demand for air traffic. There are two main terminals, as well as a first class terminal used by Lufthansa. **Munich Airport** (MUC) is the second busiest airport in Germany and provides access to the region of Bavaria. It is located about 28.5km northeast of the historical part of Munich. **Düsseldorf Airport** (DUS) is the 3rd busiest airport in Germany and provides access to the sprawling metropolis of the Rhine-Ruhr Region. It lies about 7km north of Düsseldorf and 20km from Essen. **Hamburg Airport** (HAM) is the 5th busiest airport in Germany. Located about 8.5km north of the center of Hamburg, it provides access to the north of

BERLIN TRAVEL GUIDE

Germany. **Stuttgart Airport** (STR) is located about 13km from the city of Stuttgart. It is an important base for Germanwings and provides connections to several European cities, as well as Atlanta in the USA and Abu Dhabi. **Cologne Bonn Airport** (CGN) provides access to Cologne, the 4th largest city in Germany and Bonn, former capital of West Germany. Founded as a military airfield in 1913, it was opened to civilian aviation in the early 1950s. **Nuremberg Airport** (NUE) is the second busiest airport in the region of Bavaria and provides connections between Germany and the Mediterranean, Egypt and the Canary Islands. **Leipzig/Halle Airport** (LEJ) connects travellers to Leipzig, Halle and other destinations in Saxony in the eastern part of Germany. Additionally it serves as an important cargo hub. Access to the southwest of Germany and particularly Freiburg, can also be gained via **EuroAirport Basel Mulhouse Freiburg**, (BSL) an international airport located on the border between France and Switzerland and near the border of Germany. It is operated by both countries with two additional German board members.

Airlines

Lufthansa is the largest airline in Europe and controls one of the largest passenger fleets in the world, consisting of around 280 aircrafts. It provides connections to almost 200 international destinations in 78 different countries across Europe, Africa,

BERLIN TRAVEL GUIDE

Asia and North and South America. The group was founded in 1955. Lufthansa CityLine resulted from the absorption of the regional airline, Ostfriesische Lufttaxi by Lufthansa. Air Berlin is the second largest airline in Germany and the 8th largest in Europe. Condor Flugdienst is Germany's third largest airline and is partnered with the British group Thomas Cook, as well as Lufthansa, its parent company. It flies to destinations in the Mediterranean, Asia, Africa, North and South America as well as the Caribbean. Germanwings and Eurowings are low-cost subsidiaries of Lufthansa, currently being merged and integrated into a combined enterprise. TUIfly is an airline operated by the tourism group TUI Travel. It is based at Hanover Airport with bases at several other German cities including Frankfurt, Munich, Cologne, Düsseldorf, Saarbrücken and Stuttgart. TUIfly provides connections to 39 destinations in Europe, Asia and Africa. Germania is a privately owned airline which flies to destinations within Europe, North Africa and the Middle East.

Frankfurt Airport serves as a hub for Lufthansa, Lufthansa CityLine, Condor and Aerologic. Berlin Tegel Airport serves as a hub for Air Berlin and Germanwings. Berlin Schönefeld Airport serves as a focus city for EasyJet and Condor. Düsseldorf Airport serves as a hub for Air Berlin, Eurowings and Germanwings. Munich Airport serves as a hub for Lufthansa, Lufthansa CityLine, Condor and Air Dolomiti. Stuttgart Airport also serves as a hub for Germanwings.

BERLIN TRAVEL GUIDE

Cologne Bonn Airport serves as an important European hub for UPS and FedEx Express. Additionally it is a hub for Eurowings and Germanwings. Leipzig/Halle Airport serves as a hub for Aerologic and DHL Aviation.

🌐 Currency

The currency of Germany is the Euro. It is issued in notes in denominations of €500, €200, €100, €50, €20, €10 and €5. Coins are issued in denominations of €2, €1, 50c, 20c, 10c, 5c, 2c and 1c.

🌐 Banking & ATMs

Using ATMs (Geldautomaten, as they are known in Germany), to withdraw money is simple if your ATM card is compatible with the MasterCard/Cirrus or Visa/Plus networks. Deutschebank is affiliated to Barclays, Bank of America, Scotiabank (of Canada), China Construction Bank, BNP Paribas (of France) and Westpac (of Australia and New Zealand), which means account holders of those bank groups should not be charged transaction fees when using the facilities of Deutschebank in Germany. Bear in mind that third party ATMs, however convenient, will also charge a higher transaction fee. Be sure to advise your bank of your travel plans and inquire about whether your bank card is compatible with German ATM machines.

🌐 Credit Cards

Most Germans prefer using cash when shopping and you may find the credit card option being being unavailable in many of the country's smaller shops, restaurants and guesthouses. Larger hotels and restaurants should accept credit card transactions. Shops will usually display a sign indicating which credit cards are accepted. The most popular credit cards are MasterCard, and its European affiliate, the Eurocard as well as Visa. Most German facilities are compliant with the new chip-and-pin debit and credit cards and may not be able to handle older magnetic strip cards.

🌐 Reclaiming VAT

If you are not from the European Union, you may be able to claim back VAT (Value Added Tax) paid on your purchases in Germany. The VAT rate in Germany is 19 percent and this can be claimed back on your purchases, if certain conditions are met. Only purchases of €25 and over qualify for a VAT refund. To qualify, you need to ask the shop assistant for export papers and this needs to be submitted to the Customs office at your port of exit, along with the receipt and a passport to prove residence outside the European Union. Customs officers will also want to inspect the goods in question to ascertain that they are unused. Once the export papers have been stamped, they can be sent to the shop where you bought the goods for a VAT refund. For a service fee, you can also get a cash refund from the offices of Global Blue, TaxfreeWorldwide or Premier Tax Free.

🌐 Tipping Policy

In German restaurants, you should tip your waiter around 10 percent or a little more if the service is excellent. This should be given to the waiter in cash, rather than left on the table when you depart. It is customary to tip porters in German hotels between €1 and €3 per bag. Tip your housekeeper between €3 and €5 per night and reward an unusually helpful concierge. Tip your tour guide 10 percent (although some tour guides may request a positive TripAdvisor review instead, as this translates to a cash bonus in certain tour companies), give your spa attendant 5 percent and round off a taxi fare to the nearest euro.

🌐 Mobile Phones

Germany uses the GSM mobile service. This means that most UK phones and some US and Canadian phones and mobile devices will work in Germany. However, phones using the

BERLIN TRAVEL GUIDE

CDMA network will not be compatible. While you could check with your service provider about coverage before you leave, using your own service in roaming mode will involve additional costs. The alternative is to purchase a German SIM card to use during your stay in Germany. Until recently, Germany had four mobile networks, Deutsche Telekom (formerly known as T-Mobile), Vodafone, O2 and E-plus, but the latter two, O2 and E-plus have been acquired by Telefonica and are in the process of being merged into a single brand. A huge variety of packages for different types of usage are available from representatives and subsidiaries of each of these. Deutsche Telekom has two starter pack options - data only and voice and data - from €9.95, which includes €10 credit. For the same price, you can buy a Vodafone CallYa SIM, which also offers a basic €10 credit. You can buy your E-plus SIM card from gas (petrol) stations and retail outlets from €10, with a €5 bonus credit.

🌐 Dialling Code

The international dialling code for Germany is +49.

🌐 Emergency Numbers

Police: 110
Fire Rescue: 112
Medical Emergencies: 112

BERLIN TRAVEL GUIDE

Master Card: 0800 819 1040

Visa: 0800 811 8440

🌐 Public Holidays

1 January: New Year's Day

6 January: Day of the Epiphany

March/April: Good Friday

March/April: Easter Monday

1 May: Labour Day

May: Ascension Day

May: Whit Monday

May/June: Corpus Christi

3 October: Day of German Unity

31 October: Day of Reformation

1 November: All Saints Day

25 December: Christmas Day

26 December: St Stephen's Day

🌐 Time Zone

In the winter season from the end of October to the end of March, Germany's official time zone is Central European Time, which is Greenwich Mean Time/Coordinated Universal Time (GMT/UTC) +1; Eastern Standard Time (North America) -5; Pacific Standard Time (North America) -8.

BERLIN TRAVEL GUIDE

🌎 Daylight Savings Time

Clocks are set forward one hour on the last Sunday of March and set back one hour on the last Sunday of October for Daylight Savings Time.

🌎 School Holidays

German school holidays are not determined nationally and vary from state to state. The academic year begins early in September and ends in mid July. There is a weeklong autumn break towards the end of October, a two-week winter vacation that includes Christmas and New Year, a short spring vacation in February and a short summer half term vacation at the beginning of June. After the end of the summer term in mid July, there is a longer vacation that lasts until the next school year begins in September.

🌎 Trading Hours

German department stores are generally open from 10am to 8pm, from Mondays to Saturdays, while supermarkets are open from 8am to 8pm from Monday to Saturdays. Most German shops are closed on Sundays and also on Christmas, Easter and Public Holidays. German banks are open from 8.30am to 4pm from Mondays to Fridays. Most of the gas stations in large

BERLIN TRAVEL GUIDE

urban areas and near the autobahns are open 24 hours. Museums, tourist attractions, trains and buses maintain a limited schedule on Sundays.

🌐 Driving Laws

The Germans drive on the right hand side of the road as in the USA. A driver's licence from any of the European Union member countries is valid in Germany. If you are resident of a non-EU country, you may drive on that country's license for the first six months of your stay in Germany. You may need to obtain a German translation of your driving license. The minimum driving age in Germany is 18, but most car rental companies will require renters to be at least 21. Bear in mind that the majority of cars will be stick (manual) shift and that an automatic car may be more expensive to hire. You will need to have a Green Insurance certificate as well as standard on board emergency gear like emergency triangles, a jack, spare wheel and first aid kit. German autobahns or freeways are famous for imposing no speed limit, though you may find that variable speed limits are imposed on certain sections of the road, or a 130km limit may apply where safety and congestion is a factor. At the approach of a major junction or intersection, the limit drops to 80km per hour. In urban and residential areas, the speed limit will be between 30 and 50km per hour. You will need a special sticker or Umweltplakette (which costs €6) to be

BERLIN TRAVEL GUIDE

able to drive in designated Green Zones. A violation of this policy may incur a fine of €40.

🌐 Smoking Laws

Germany has banned smoking from all indoor public places including restaurants and bars, although it is usually allowed in outdoor sections, such as beer gardens. While some businesses have obtained exemption in states such as Saxony, Rhineland-Pfalz and Saarland, the regulations are particularly strict in Bavaria. Fines vary according to region, but can be anything from €10 to €5000. To buy cigarettes from a vending machine, you will be required to submit some form of identification.

🌐 Drinking Laws

The legal drinking age in Germany is 16, although minors can consume beer or wine from the age of 14, if in the company of a parent or guardian. They can, however, only consume and buy distilled beverages, such as whiskey and brandy, from the age of 18. In general, Germany enjoys some of the most lenient laws towards alcohol consumption and public drinking is mostly tolerated. Some places forbid the consumption of alcohol on trains and transit. Alcohol can be bought from a variety of places including restaurants, bars, grocery stores,

BERLIN TRAVEL GUIDE

garages and even newspaper vendors. Additionally the price of alcohol is the lowest in Europe.

🌐 Electricity

Electricity: 230 volts

Frequency: 50 Hz

German electricity sockets use the Type C and F plugs, which feature two round pins or prongs. If travelling from the USA, you will need a power converter or transformer to convert the voltage from 230 to 110, to avoid damage to your appliances. The latest models of many laptops, camcorders, mobile phones and digital cameras are dual-voltage with a built in converter.

🌐 Tourist Information (TI)

There are Tourist and Visitor Information offices in several of the larger German cities, where you can pick up maps and local travel guides to help plan your visit. The Berlin office is at 11 Am Karlsbad; in Frankfurt, go to 56 Kaiserstrasse; in Hamburg, 7 Steinstrasse; in Munich, 1 Sendlinger Strasse; in Leipzig, 1 Richard Wagner Strasse; in Stuttgart, 1 Königstrasse; in Hannover, 8 Ernst-August-Platz; in Dusseldorf, 65b Immermannstrasse; in Bonn, 131 Adenauerallee; in Cologne, 19 Unter Fettenhennen; in Nuremberg, 3 Frauentorgraben; in Dresden, 11 Ostra-Allee and in Dortmund, 18a Königswall.

BERLIN TRAVEL GUIDE

🌍 Food & Drink

There are well over 1500 different types of sausage (wurst) made in Germany. These are divided into four basic types - raw wurst, cooked wurst, scalded wurst and, of course, the famous bratwurst, which can be found in over 50 regional varieties. Wienerwurst is a relative of the American frankfurter, but do not confuse the American frankfurter with the German one, a smoked sausage of pure pork which is regional speciality of the city of Frankfurt. There is also a good selection of raw and cooked ham, known locally as schinken. With 400 different types of cheese, dairy lovers will also be spoilt for choice, especially in the pre-alpine region of Allgäu in Bavaria, which produces the majority of the country's cheeses. A traditional German stew is eintopf, so named as it is prepared in a single pot. Enjoy Berlin cuisine with a delicious helping of eisbein, pickled ham hock served with sauerkraut or mashed potatoes. On the sweet side, apfelstrudel is a popular German pastry made with apples, cinnamon and raisins. If you are in Germany around Christmas time, spoil yourself with a helping of seasonal lebkuchen.

German drinking culture is synonymous with beer. The country has around 1200 breweries and more than 5000 different beer brands. In most parts of Germany, pale lager pilsner is the preferred beer, although wheat (weiss) beer is popular in Bavaria. Try a dark beer known as Altbier from Düsseldorf. As an after dinner digestive, Germans enjoy Schnapps, a clear, strong fruit-flavored alcoholic drink or herbal liqueurs such as Jägermeister and Underberg. Germany has some decent wine varietals from grapes that are grown along the banks of the Rheine and the Mosel. For a novelty, try an Eiswein (ice wine), a sweet dessert wine produced from grapes that were frozen while still on the vine. Apfelwein or cider is a popular alternative to beer and can be combined with sparkling water for Sauer Gespritzer or lemonade for Sussgespritzer. A local variety from Frankfurt called Speierling adds berries to the usual apfelwein. On the non-alcoholic side, Germans are also fond of fruit juice and mix this with sparkling water, especially apple juice. This particular mix is known as apfelschorle. Additionally, Germans love strong, flavorful coffee, which is hardly surprising since the coffee filter was invented in Germany.

Websites

http://www.germany.travel/en/index.html

http://www.german-way.com/

http://www.howtogermany.com/

http://www.germany-tourism.net/

BERLIN TRAVEL GUIDE

https://www.deutschland.de/en/topic/life/mobility-travel/tourism

http://germanyiswunderbar.com/

http://wikitravel.org/en/Germany

Manufactured by Amazon.ca
Bolton, ON